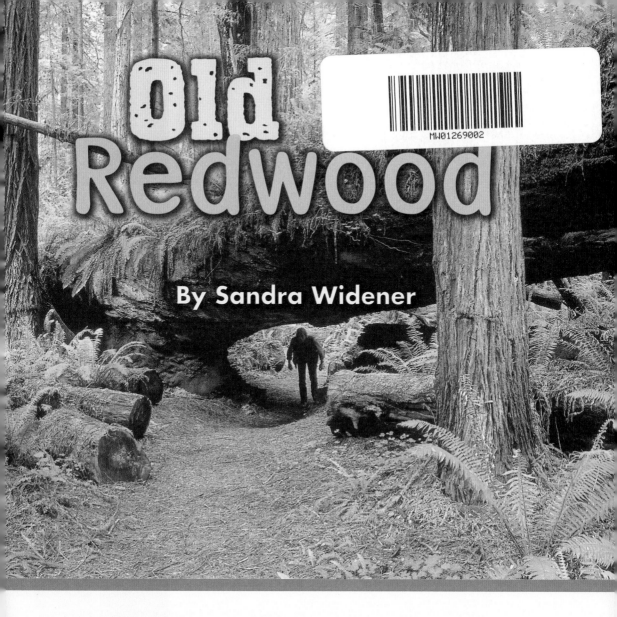

Old Redwood

By Sandra Widener

In this book, you will read about the tallest trees on Earth. As you read, think about the ways in which these trees are special.

PEARSON

Contents

California Redwoods

Did you know that some trees in California and Oregon can grow taller than 350 feet? That's about as tall as a building with 35 floors! These trees are called coast redwoods. Coast redwoods are the tallest trees on Earth. They grow near the coast of the Pacific Ocean.

Not only are they tall, coast redwoods can live a long time, too. One coast redwood lived for more than 2,000 years. These trees are some of the oldest living things on Earth.

Coast redwoods are among the fastest-growing trees.

GENERAL SHERMAN

4

⬢ Coast redwoods belong in the redwood family. The giant sequoia (seh-KWOI-uh) is another tree in the redwood family. Giant sequoias live even longer than coast redwoods. One giant sequoia lived for more than 3,000 years!

⬤ The giant sequoia doesn't grow as tall as the coast redwood. But the trunk of the giant sequoia can be much larger. The distance around the trunk of the largest giant sequoia is more than 102 feet!

⬤ The General Sherman is the largest living giant sequoia. The trunk might weigh almost as much as 15 blue whales!

5

The Story of a Redwood

Groves of redwood trees grew during the time of the dinosaurs. Those trees are no longer alive. However, there are many redwood trees alive today. Some of these redwoods grew from seeds.

Redwood trees make many seed cones. Inside the cones are lots of seeds. As the wind blows through a **grove**, the seed cones shake. The seeds blow away from the cones.

⬤ The seed cone of a coast redwood is about the size of an olive.

Very few of the seeds will grow into trees. Most of the seeds will not reach the soil. Some seeds will land in water. Other seeds will be eaten by animals.

Let's think about a tree that could have started growing along the California coast a long time ago.

First, suppose that a seed landed on the ground about 2,000 years ago. Now, suppose the seed became covered with soil. It received the water it needed. Before long, the seed grew into a small coast redwood tree.

Redwood seeds are tiny. It would take many redwood seeds to cover the surface of a penny.

The Redwood Grows

A tiny tree is called a **seedling**. The California coast has mild weather. There are foggy and rainy days. There are also warm and sunny days. Sunlight along with water from rain and fog help seedlings grow.

Let's suppose our **seedling** got plenty of rain. It grew quickly and became a tall tree. When our tree was 3 years old, it was about 6 feet tall. When our tree was 75 years old, it was about 120 feet tall.

50 feet

25 feet

6 feet

3 years old

12 years old

20 years old

120 feet

100 feet

50 years
old

75 years
old

11

 By the time our tree was 500 years old, it was about 200 feet tall. A coast redwood can grow several feet in one year if it gets enough water and sunlight.

A coast redwood's **bark** is a deep red-brown color. This color is what gives the redwood tree its name.

The **bark** of a coast redwood tree protects the tree. The bark of a coast redwood can be 12 inches thick. It does not burn easily. Bugs cannot get through the bark.

Coast redwoods can grow from seeds or sprouts. Sprouts are young plants that can grow from tree roots.

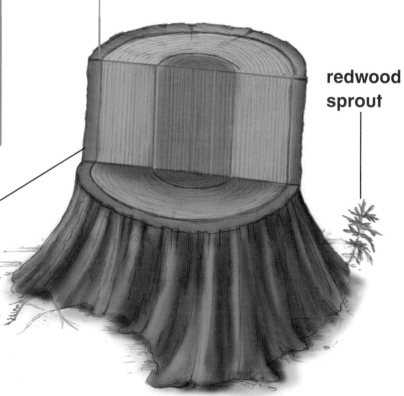

bark

redwood sprout

People and the Redwood

When our coast redwood tree was 1,000 years old, it was still growing. The grove where it was growing had many other redwood trees. Native Americans used the redwoods for shade. Native Americans also used redwood **lumber** to make boats and houses.

Native Americans used redwood boats to hunt and fish.

Native Americans knew that **lumber** from a redwood tree lasts a long time. Bugs, water, and fire do not easily hurt redwood.

Native Americans used redwood to build houses like the one shown here.

DETROIT PHOTOGRAPHIC CO., PUBLISHERS

7493· BIG

16

When our tree was 1,800 years old it was almost 300 feet tall. **Settlers** came to California to look for gold. Around the tree, other redwoods were cut down to build homes for the settlers.

Some redwood trees took three or more days to cut down. One tree made enough lumber to build several houses for the **settlers**.

Settlers looked for gold in California's streams and rivers.

This old postcard from 1900 shows big redwoods in California.

The loads of redwood on this train may have come from one redwood tree!

18

 Redwoods Today

Suppose our coast redwood tree is still alive. It is now 2,000 years old. It has lived through forest fires and floods. It is taller than the Statue of Liberty in New York City. The bottom of the tree's trunk is about 70 feet around.

Here's a way to picture the size of the trunk. Count out 70 feet on a string. Then make a circle with the string. Walk around the circle to see the great size of the redwood's trunk.

People pay a fee to drive through this coast redwood tree.

Years ago, people began to understand that redwoods are special. Now there are several parks in California where these trees are protected. **Loggers** cannot cut down the trees in these parks.

In other places, **loggers** cut down redwoods for lumber. Redwood is good lumber for building.

Even with powerful tools, it can take a whole day to cut down a redwood tree.

Today, our 2,000-year-old coast redwood tree could be part of Redwood National Park in California. Our tree could be among the many trees that thousands of visitors come to see. The visitors look up hundreds of feet to see some of the most amazing trees on Earth.

In this park, winds blow. Seeds fly from seed cones. New seeds land on the ground. New redwoods start to grow.

Looking up, you can barely see the tops of redwood trees.

Redwood is used to build playgrounds.

Glossary

bark the outer covering of a tree

grove a group of trees

loggers people whose work is to cut down trees

lumber wood that has been sawed so that it can be used for building

seedling a new plant that has roots, a stem, and leaves

settlers people who set up their life in a new place